Read It!
Draw It!
Solve It!

PROBLEM SOLVING FOR PRIMARY GRADES
TEACHER RESOURCE BOOK

Elizabeth D. Miller

GRADE ONE

Dale Seymour Publications®

Managing Editor: Catherine Anderson
Product Manager: Lois Fowkes
Senior Editor: Jeri Hayes
Project Editor: Julie Carlson
Production/Manufacturing Director: Janet Yearian
Senior Production Coordinator: Alan Noyes
Design Manager: Jeff Kelly
Cover Design: Alison Jewett-Furlo / Square Moon Productions
Cover Illustration: Stan Tusan / Square Moon Productions
Text Design: Square Moon Productions

Dale Seymour Publications® is an imprint of Addison Wesley Longman, Inc.

This Book Is Printed
On Recycled Paper

ISBN 1-57232-434-1
Order number DS33800
1 2 3 4 5 6 7 8 9 10 -ML- 01 00 99 98 97

Why This Program Was Created

Read It! Draw It! Solve It! is a unique problem-solving program designed for children from reading readiness through third grade. It was created to increase young children's understanding of mathematical concepts through direct visual involvement. For each problem in the program, students will demonstrate their understanding of the concept by creating a drawing before providing the answer.

Students who use this program become confident in their reasoning abilities and are able to communicate easily their understanding of mathematics. When young children work with illustrations they have made rather than abstract symbols, they learn to think of mathematics as problem solving rather than rote learning. They learn to reason rather than simply react, and they develop a better understanding of what they are doing. They also learn to read carefully because they know that they will have to demonstrate their understanding with a drawing.

Students love the open-endedness of the problems. The program encourages creativity in thought and expression, and it celebrates diversity. No two drawings will ever be the same, and many of the problems lend themselves to a variety of solutions.

Moreover, when students illustrate problems, the teacher gets a better understanding of their thought processes. If an answer is incorrect, it is usually easy to tell from the drawing where the student went wrong. Given the problem, "Nine people have come to the dance. Can everyone have a partner?" one boy made a picture of nine happy people in a row and answered "Yes." He had read the question as, "Can everyone have a party?" When his teacher helped him to read the problem correctly, he altered his illustration and answered "no."

How to Use This Book

Each book contains 180 problems, one for each day of the school year. The routine is the same throughout the program, although at the beginning of the year you will want to be sure to follow the activity with a discussion period to be sure any questions are answered fully.

Your task at the first-grade level is to lead the group in learning how to read and understand the words. You will also need to be sure that students know they are to draw the picture before trying to solve the problem. Discussion at this stage is critically important, so that students will feel supported and will build their confidence in working more independently. As the year progresses, you can divide the class

Samples of Student Work

by Jenna Cannavaro

2 hornets stung Harry.
Brad got stung by that many plus 2 more.
Brad is very sore.

How many hornets stung Brad? 4

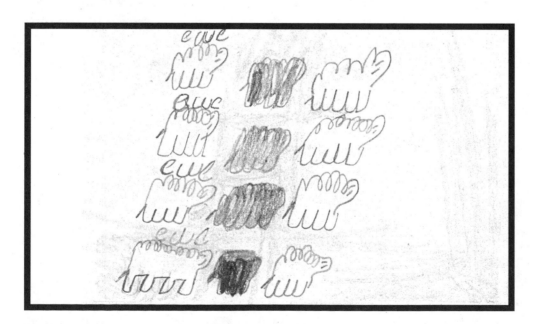

by Catie Connolly

Each ewe had 1 black lamb and 1 white lamb.
There were 4 ewes.

How many black lambs were there? 4

into small groups or pairs or even try individual work. The goal is to encourage creativity while being responsive to these young thinkers' needs.

You may want to use this program as it was set up—one problem a day—or you may want to pick and choose problems according to the needs of your students and how they fit into your other curriculum areas. Note, however, that the problems increase in reading and mathematical difficulty over the course of the year.

Read It! Draw It! Solve It! can be integrated with any math or reading program. A blank template is provided for you on page xi to make up special problems for your class that incorporate specific information your students are learning.

Also offered in this set is an animal themes program with 45 problems each for kindergarten through third grade. These exercises require students to demonstrate understanding of animal attributes as well as math concepts, and provide an intriguing supplement to animal studies units that you may be doing at any of these grade levels.

What Your Students Will Learn

READING

Read It! Draw It! Solve It! was originally created for first graders. It was designed not only to encourage real understanding of mathematical concepts, but also to provide texts for beginning readers.

Reading instruction may be divided into three stages. The first stage is reading readiness. The second stage is the "decoding" stage. The third stage is the "reading comprehension stage." At this third stage, a person reads for knowledge and for pleasure.

Most first graders have gone through some sort of reading readiness program and are ready to begin learning to decode. In order to get meaning from a paragraph, one must be able to identify the individual words. In other words, you cannot know what the word means if you do not know what the word says. Proper use of a systematic phonetic reading program will teach most students, regardless of background, to correctly identify most of the words within their comprehension vocabularies.

Although it may be used in conjunction with any reading program, *Read It! Draw It! Solve It!* was intended to dovetail with a specific program developed for systematic phonics instruction. Letters appearing next to the page numbers indicate the sound that is being taught on those days. The early problems contain only short vowel sounds and single consonant words. Students progress to consonant blends and digraphs, and then through long and variant vowels. In the last part of the first grade program the problems contain words full of English spelling irregularities.

Some students will be afraid to try to draw at the beginning of the year. It is important to start slowly and to praise whatever efforts they make. Confidence comes with practice. The first few problems at least should be done only after a lot of discussion with the whole class. In this way, your students will learn that whatever appears in the problem must be represented in the illustration. Show them that an inaccurate illustration will produce an incorrect answer.

Young children can use art to communicate. They can expand and enjoy their drawing abilities while doing math that, in regular textbooks, might seem too difficult. Here is an opportunity to learn math concepts while learning to read and communicate in a fun way.

Right from the start, you can also encourage your students, by example and through discussion, to appreciate diversity. Let the children see that no two illustrations are alike, and let them learn to appreciate each other's interpretations. As the year progresses, you might want to break up into small groups or pairs for discussion, or ask them to work on some of the problems individually.

The vocabulary in this program is developed systematically, from consistently spelled words like *bat* and *tin*, through long vowel sound words like *see* and *sea*, to more difficult words like *lamb* and *chandelier*.

- Lessons 1 through 19 use short vowel sound words with single consonants.

- Lessons 20 through 45 continue with short vowel sounds, and introduce consonant blends and digraphs. J, Z, and the consonant sound of Y are also introduced here.

- Lessons 46 through 67 contain common short vowel sounds, the long i sound of Y, and consonants V and QU.

- Lessons 68 through 90 reintroduces all sounds previously taught, now presented in two- and three-syllable words.

- Lessons 91 through 135 contain words with variant vowels such as oo, oi, ir, and ar.

- Lessons 136 through 180 contain words with atypical spelling patterns such as ph = f, ch = k, gh, and ough.

A student using this system will progress from reading simple words that he can spell as well as read to reading the unusually spelled but commonly used words that make English such a difficult language.

Spend a lot of time with first graders as each problem is introduced. Make sure that they can read the words, and that they know what the words mean.

MATH

At the first-grade level, students work with numbers from zero to ten. After they complete this program they will have a genuine understanding of these numbers and have a solid basis for the study of more advanced mathematics. They will encounter these numbers in all kinds of situations. They will do addition, subtraction, multiplication, and division exercises, and even work with fractions.

At this level children become comfortable with drawing as a means of informing and as an enjoyable form of self-expression. They take great pride in their work. Adults looking at the illustrations will come to a much better understanding of each child as an individual.

On the first day of first grade the problem is:

I cat and I cat
How many cats?

Some children will be able to read, but many will not. Group reading will ensure that everyone knows what the words say, and what they mean. What must appear in the picture in order to present the correct answer? Some children may be timid about drawing, and this is a time for great encouragement and for appreciation of each child's work. As they do this every day, confidence will build and drawings will become more sophisticated.

Concepts and vocabulary increase in difficulty as the year progresses. On the sixtieth day, students are asked to do the following problem:

There are 5 seats on the train.
9 men ride on the train.

How many men have to stand?

By this time in the year there will be some advanced students who prefer to proceed without teacher assistance. However, for some, group reading and discussion is still essential. What must appear in the picture? We must show 5 seats, and then we must draw 9 men, allowing 5 of them to sit down and leaving the rest standing.

By day 143 where the daily problem is:

How many shoes must you buy for a set of quintuplets?

almost all of the students will be able to work independently, providing they can read the words and know what quintuplets are.

On the other hand, the problem for day 152

The cylinder on the left is 5 inches tall.
The cylinder on the right is twice as tall.

How tall is the cylinder on the right?

is much better handled as a group activity.

The chart below shows the skill featured in each problem:

MATH CONCEPTS FOR FIRST GRADE MASTERY	PAGES WITH PRACTICE PROBLEMS
addition and subtraction	1–6, 8–18, 20, 22–24, 26–30, 32–39, 41–61, 65, 69, 74, 77, 81, 82, 89, 90–93, 97, 99, 100, 101, 104, 105, 107, 114, 115, 116, 118, 119, 120, 123, 126, 129, 130, 133, 134, 135, 136, 139, 140, 142, 144, 146, 147, 149, 151, 155, 158, 160, 161, 162, 174, 178
multiplication	62, 66, 67, 73, 75, 76, 80, 83, 84, 85, 94, 95, 98, 109, 113, 143
division	111, 112, 125, 127, 131, 138, 145, 154, 163, 165, 169, 170, 175
vocabulary	21, 40, 70, 71, 72, 78, 79, 121, 128, 148, 152, 157, 159, 164, 167, 180
order and patterns	7, 19, 25, 31, 106, 173
equivalence	68, 87, 88, 96, 102, 103, 108, 124, 132, 137, 141, 153, 172, 176, 179
measurement	117, 150
fractions	110, 122, 166, 168, 171
shapes	63, 64, 86, 156, 177

Analyzing delightful illustrations is a lot more fun for a teacher than simply correcting papers. More important, the analysis helps the teacher to better understand individual thought processes, and then to provide appropriate encouragement and assistance. The better a teacher understands each student, the higher will be student success rate.

Instead of "training" students in specific strategies, this program educates young people to discover what it takes to solve any kind of problem. Because of this approach, students are not intimidated when confronted with novel situations. They learn to look for more than one way to solve a problem—and sometimes, for more than one answer. Perhaps the most exciting aspect of this program is that as students develop confidence in their reasoning abilities they take this confidence with them into other areas of the curriculum.

Blank Template

Use the template on the next page to provide your students with special problems that pertain to the work they are doing.

Name _____

I cat and I cat.

How many cats? _____

cats
_____
- -
_____

2 cats on a mat.
I cat off the mat.

How many cats? _____

mat

_____

- -

_____

3 nests and 2 nests.

How many nests? _____

nests

_____

- -

_____

Dan has 2 pans.
Dad has 2 pans.

How many pans? _____

Dad

_____

- -

_____

3 tags on the big pan.
0 tags on the little pan.

How many tags? _____

tags

_____

- -

_____

3 big maps.
2 little maps.

How many maps? _____

maps
_____
- -
_____

[empty box]

Make pictures of a man, a pig, and a pup.

Which one doesn't belong? _____

Why? _____

_____

Ann has 4 bats.
Nan has 0 bats.

How many bats? _____

bats

_____

- -

_____

```



```

1 bug is in the sun.
4 bugs sit in the mud.

How many bugs? _____

bugs

_____

- -

_____

5 hats sit in a pit.
Sam digs up 1 hat.

How many hats still sit in the pit? _____

sit

_____

- -

_____

4 eggs sat in a pan.
2 eggs fell out.

How many eggs still sit in the pan? _____

eggs _____

- -

_____

3 rats sat on a mat.
2 rats ran away.

How many rats still sit on the mat? _____

rats

_____

- -

_____

5 fat pets sat in a pen.
Dan fed 4 pets.

How many pets did not get fed? _____

fed

_____

- -

_____

Ron has 5 balloons.
3 balloons pop.

How many balloons are left? _____

pop
_____

- -

_____

```




```

A man has 5 dolls.
The man sells 5 dolls.

How many dolls are left? _____

dolls
_____
- -
_____

He has 4 hats.
He hid 3 hats.

How many hats does he have now? _____

hats

_____

- -

_____

5 cats sit in a cab.
2 cats get out.

How many cats are left? _____

cab
_____
- -
_____

4 chicks sit on a mat.
Kim picks up 1 chick.

How many chicks are left on the mat? _____

chicks

_____

- -

_____

Make pictures of a box, a fox, a box, and a fox.

What comes next? _____

box

_____

- -

_____

6 ducks swim in a tank.
5 ducks sink.

How many ducks still swim? _____

ducks
_____

- -

_____

Glen has a big flag.

The top half of the flag is red.
The bottom half of the flag is green.

flag

_____

- -

_____

Jauna builds with 3 blocks.
Sam builds with 3 blocks.

How many blocks? _____

blocks

_____

- -

_____

6 crabs sat on a drum.
3 crabs got off the drum.

How many crabs are left on the drum? _____

drum

[blank drawing box]

Brianne had 6 drums on a truck.
Greg put 6 drums from the truck onto a train.

How many drums are left on the truck? _____

truck

_____

- -

_____

Make pictures of a frog, a crab, and a crib.

Which 2 go together? _____

Why? _____

_____

_____

Lester stacks 3 blocks.
Stan adds 5 blocks.

How many blocks are in the stack? _____

stack

_____

- -

_____

7 snakes rest on the rocks.
I snake slithers away.
The rest of the snakes stay.

How many snakes stay? _____

snakes

----

8 skunks.
4 snacks.

How many skunks have no snacks? _____

skunks

_____

- -

_____

8 students.
6 students have smocks.
The rest get spots on their shirts.

How many students have spots on their shirts? _____

shirts
_____
- -
_____

4 tops sit still.
5 tops spin.

How many tops? _____

spin

_____

- -

_____

Make a picture of one black ant and two red crabs.
Underneath it make a picture of one red ant.
Put two crabs next to the ant.

What color will the crabs be? _____

ants

_____

_____

9 lamps at camp.
2 lamps went out.

How many lamps are still lit? _____

lamps

_____

- -

_____

6 frogs swim in the pond.
2 frogs sit on the sand.

How many frogs? _____

pond
_____
- -
_____

2 sets of twins swim.

How many children? _____

twins

_____

- -

_____

Jess and Jed jog.
Jim and Jill jump.
Jeff and Jen just sit.

How many children? _____

jog

3 zebras in the zoo.
2 yaks.

How many animals are in the zoo? _____

yaks, zoo

_____

- -

_____

9 fish swim in a dish.
7 fish are red.
The rest are black.

How many fish are black? _____

fish

_____

- -

_____

[blank drawing box]

Chet chops 6 logs.
Chad chops 2 more logs than Chet chops.

How many logs does Chad chop? _____

chop

_____

- -

_____

8 sticks block the path.
4 sticks are thick.
The rest are thin.

How many sticks are thin? _____

thin
_____
- -
_____

Make a big rectangle.

The left half is green.
The right half is blue.

rectangle _____

_____

---

8 students in class.
Half of the students sit.
Half of the students stand and clap.

How many students stand and clap? _____

clap

_____

- -

_____

9 imps.
4 imps spill milk.
The rest mop it up.

How many imps mop? _____

imps

_____

- -

_____

3 rugs.
2 bugs under each rug.

How many bugs? _____

rugs _____

- -

_____

7 tots.
Some tots have socks on.
5 tots have socks off.

How many tots have socks on? _____

tots
_____

- -

_____

6 hens.
Some hens sit on eggs.
2 hens have no eggs.

How many hens have eggs? _____

hens
_____
- -
_____

9 balloons.
5 balloons fly in the sky.
The rest go into the pond.

How many balloons go into the pond? _____

sky

_____

- -

_____

Here are some planes.
6 are in the sky.
2 are on land.

How many planes in all? _____

planes
_____
- -
_____

8 kids are on the slide.
Some go up the slide.
2 go down the slide.

How many kids go up the slide? _____

slide

_____

- -

_____

Shani has 7 pals.
Shani sent notes to some of them.
4 pals got notes.

How many pals did not get notes? _____

notes
_____

- -

_____

6 cubes are in a pile.
Jake takes some cubes.
2 cubes are left.

How many cubes did Jake take? _____

cubes

_____

- -

_____

Pete fed 2 cats, 3 dogs, and 4 fish.

How many pets did Pete feed? _____

feed

_____

- -

_____

(empty drawing box)

3 peaches are ready to eat.
6 peaches are not yet ready.

How many peaches? _____

eat

_____

- -

_____

Gail hooks 2 cars onto the train.
Tanya adds 4 cars.
José adds 3 cars.

How many cars are on the train? _____

train
_____
- -
_____

I toad hops.
7 toads sleep.

How many toads? _____

toad

_____

- -

_____

[blank drawing box]

A hen lays 9 eggs in the hay.
Some eggs are okay.
5 eggs broke.

How many eggs are okay? _____

hay
_____
- -
_____

I tree is green.
4 trees are red.
2 trees are yellow.

How many trees? _____

trees

_____

- -

_____

Dean has some beans.
Jean eats 5 beans.
2 beans are left.

How many beans did Dean have to begin with? _____

beans
_____

- -

_____

9 vases sit on the table.
Val takes 5 vases.

How many vases are left? _____

vases

_____

- -

_____

8 men sit in a boat.
To float, the boat can only hold 6 men.

How many men need to get off the boat? _____

boat _____

- -

_____

There are 5 seats on the train.
9 men ride on the train.

How many men have to stand? _____

train

_____

- -

_____

9 whales swim in the sea.

3 whales are black.

The rest of the whales are white.

How many whales are white? _____

whales

_____

- -

_____

3 men slowly row a big boat.
Each man has 2 oars.

How many oars are in the boat? _____

slowly

_____

- -

_____

Make a picture of four squares.

Put a squirrel to the left of the first square.
Put a squirrel to the right of the second square.
Put a squirrel over the third square.
Put a squirrel under the fourth square.

square
_____

- -

_____

Make a shape with sides.

Draw an apple inside the shape.
Put three black dots in the middle of the apple.

shape

_____

- -

_____

We have 5 kids and 3 bikes.

How many more bikes do we need? _____

bikes

_____

- -

_____

Rosy has 3 trucks.
Each truck tows 2 boats.

How many boats can Rosy tow? _____

tow

_____

- -

_____

Every sheep in the pen can eat 3 piles of feed.
We have 2 sheep.

How many piles of feed do we need? _____

sheep _____

- -

_____

Ann has 5 beanbags.
Nan has 1 black beanbag and 3 red ones.
Dot has 2 black beanbags and 2 red ones.
Fran has 3 black beanbags and 2 red ones.

Who has the same number of beanbags as Ann?

```
┌─────────────────────────────────────────────────┐
│                                                 │
│                                                 │
│                                                 │
│                                                 │
│                                                 │
│                                                 │
│                                                 │
│                                                 │
│                                                 │
│                                                 │
│                                                 │
│                                                 │
└─────────────────────────────────────────────────┘
```

Mom has 7 cupcakes on a tray.
Grandma's tray has 2 more cupcakes than Mom's has.

How many cupcakes are on Grandma's tray? _____

cupcakes

_____

- -

_____

We need 5 kids for a basketball team.
We have 4 kids.

How many more kids do we need? _____

basketball

_____

- -

_____

Max, Tom, and Sam have a contest.
Max is the fastest.
Sam is the slowest.

Who arrives first? _____

Who arrives last? _____

Jared planted 5 bean plants and 3 pepper plants.
Hank planted 2 bean plants and 4 pepper plants.
Achmed planted 1 bean plant and 6 pepper plants.

Who planted the most plants? _____

Grandpa baked cupcakes.
He gave the cupcakes to Ben, Bess, and Bill.
Each of them ate 2 cupcakes.
All the cupcakes were eaten.

How many cupcakes did Grandpa bake? _____

cupcakes
_____

- -

_____

Len and Peg went fishing.
Len got 5 fish.
Peg got 1 more fish than Len got.

How many fish did Peg get? _____

fishing

_____

- -

_____

2 kids are raking leaves.
Each child has to rake 3 piles of leaves.

How many piles of leaves will they have? _____

raking
_____
- -
_____

4 whales swim in the sea.
2 little fish are swimming next to each whale.

How many little fish are there? _____

swimming
_____
- -
_____

Jésus ate 3 pancakes.

Russ ate 1 more pancake than Jésus ate.

Rachel didn't eat any pancakes.

How many pancakes were eaten? _____

didn't

_____

- -

_____

The little tree has 3 apples.
The bigger tree has 5 apples.
The biggest tree has 2 apples.

How many apples? _____

apples

_____

- -

_____

There are 9 rungs on the ladder.
Yolanda is on the third rung.
Elena is 3 rungs higher than Yolanda.

What number rung is Elena on? _____

ladder

_____

- -

_____

4 men are playing tennis.
Each man holds 2 tennis balls.

How many balls are there? _____

tennis

_____

- -

_____

Some dogs were playing in a kennel.
5 dogs jumped out of the kennel.
3 dogs are left in the kennel.

How many dogs were there to begin with? _____

kennel

_____

- -

_____

Tim has 3 lemons and 4 melons.
Van has 2 lemons and 3 melons.
Wes has 1 lemon and 7 melons.

Who has the most fruit? _____

Who has the least? _____

3 people go on a picnic.
Each one uses 2 napkins.
Each one eats 3 drumsticks.

How many napkins? _____

How many drumsticks? _____

My sisters and I are triplets.

How many dinners do we need? _____

How many mittens do we need? _____

triplets
_____

- -

_____

It takes 2 pilots to fly each big airplane.
4 airplanes are ready for takeoff.

How many pilots do we need? _____

pilots _____

_____

We are jumping on circles on the playground.
Hannah is on the third circle.
Marta is on the fifth circle.
Jomel is on the one in between.

Which circle is Jomel on? _____

playground

_____

- -

_____

Franklin has 2 orange papers and 1 yellow one.
Betsy has the same number of papers as Franklin.

How many papers does Betsy have? _____

papers

_____

- -

_____

Marcía traded trailers with Chen.
She gave Chen 3 red trailers and 4 blue ones.
She wants to get an equal number of trailers back.

How many trailers must Chen give her? _____

trailers

_____

- -

_____

9 children are at a Halloween party.
2 are dressed as chimpanzees.
3 are dressed as butterflies.
The rest are dressed as clowns.

How many children are dressed as clowns? _____

butterflies
_____
- -
_____

[blank box]

Some rattlesnakes sit in the sun.
3 rattlesnakes are eating.
4 are sleeping.

How many rattlesnakes are there? _____

rattlesnakes
_____

- -

_____

A gray squirrel had 5 walnuts in his nest.
A red squirrel had 2 more walnuts than
the gray squirrel had.

How many walnuts did the red squirrel have? _____

walnuts

_____

- -

_____

A big fish swam in a tank with 8 goldfish.
The big fish ate some of the goldfish.
3 goldfish were left.

How many goldfish did the big fish eat? _____

goldfish
_____

- -

_____

Kate and Tanya find 3 blocks to build with.
Lupita and Rolanda find 4 blocks.

How many blocks did everyone find? _____

build

_____

- -

_____

This small parking lot holds only 10 cars.
The parking lot is divided into 5 parts.

How many cars can park in each part? _____

park _____

_____

Each doe has 1 fawn.
We see 7 does.

How many fawns do we see? _____

fawn _____

- -

_____

Mort has 3 black horses and 2 white horses.
Gordon has an equal number of horses.

How many horses does Gordon have? _____

horses

_____

- -

_____

[blank box]

Barbara picked 3 red flowers, 2 purple flowers,
and 1 pink one.
She gave Kim 2 red flowers and 1 purple one.

How many flowers does Barbara have left? _____

flowers
_____

- -

_____

Dad boils water for hot chocolate.
4 boys each want to drink 2 cups of hot chocolate.

How much water must Dad boil? _____

boil

_____

- -

_____

Beth has read 3 books this week.
Yoko has read 4 more books than Beth has read.

How many books has Yoko read? _____

books

_____

- -

_____

My baby has 1 upper tooth.
Soon he will have 1 upper tooth and 1 lower one.

How many teeth will he have? _____

tooth

_____

- -

_____

┌───┐
│   │
│   │
│   │
│   │
│   │
│   │
│   │
│   │
│   │
└───┘

9 people have come to breakfast.
Each one is waiting for 1 warm waffle.
Mom has made only 7 waffles.

How many more waffles must Mom make? _____

warm

_____

- -

_____

_____

The robin has 4 babies in the nest.
She brings 8 worms back to the nest.

If each baby gets an equal number of worms,
how many worms does each baby get? _____

worms

_____

- -

_____

There are 10 squares in my quilt.
Each square has only 1 color.
The colors are red, orange, yellow, blue, and green.
There is an equal number of each color.

How many blue squares in my quilt? _____

squares _____

- -

_____

Fern ordered some desserts.
7 desserts were eaten.
2 desserts are left.

How many desserts did Fern order? _____

ordered

_____

- -

_____

Name _____

Dad gave me some balloons.
2 burst.
I still have 3 balloons.

How many balloons did Dad give me? _____

burst
_____
- -
_____

8 birds stand in a line.
Every other bird is eating birdseed.
The first, third, and fifth birds are eating birdseed.

Which other bird is eating birdseed? _____

bird

_____

- -

_____

(blank box for drawing)

Mary has 4 fuzzy chicks.
Betsy has 4 more chicks than Mary has.

How many chicks does Betsy have? _____

fuzzy _____

_____

_____

We are playing volleyball.
The red team has 5 children.
The blue team has 7 children.

How can we make the volleyball teams equal? _____

_____

volleyball
_____

- -

_____

Pro basketball teams always have 5 players.
2 teams are on the court.

How many players are on the court? _____

always

_____

- -

_____

I have 8 beautiful plants in my garden.
My garden is divided into 4 equal parts.
In 1 part the flowers are blue.
In 1 part they are scarlet.
In 1 part they are yellow.
In 1 part they are purple.

How many plants in each part? _____

part

_____

- -

_____

We are drinking milkshakes.
Each of us wants 2 straws.
There are 3 of us.

How many straws do we want? _____

straws
_____
- -
_____

Each child put 2 ornaments on the tree.
8 ornaments are on the tree.

How many children are there? _____

ornaments

_____

- -

_____

[blank box]

Sofia, Doris, and Isabel ate some corn.
Each ate 3 ears of corn.

How many ears of corn were eaten? _____

corn
_____

- -

_____

Troy had 8 coins in his pocket.
He tripped and fell, and some of the coins fell
out of his pocket.
He has 1 coin left.

How many coins did Troy lose? _____

coin

_____

- -

_____

We have 7 people coming to dinner.
Pam has to set the table.
She has 6 spoons in her hand.

How many more spoons will she need? _____

spoons

_____

_____

Wayne had 9 dollar bills in his wallet.
He spent 3 dollars at the toy store.
He spent 1 dollar at the candy store.
He bought a book for 4 dollars. He wanted to buy a kite for 2 dollars.

Did he have enough money? _____

wallet

_____

- -

_____

---

2 cups of water equal 1 pint.
2 pints equal 1 quart.

How many cups equal 1 quart? _____

water _____

- -

_____

I have 9 coins.
5 of them are dull.
The others are shiny.

How many coins are shiny? _____

shiny

_____

- -

_____

I see 3 wires with 8 birds on them.
5 birds sit on the first wire.
0 birds sit on the second wire.

How many birds sit on the third wire? _____

third
_____
- -
_____

2 hornets stung Gloria.
Norman got stung by that many plus 2 more.
Norman is very sore.

How many hornets stung Norman? _____

hornets

_____

- -

_____

Betsy is tiny. Randy is little.
Sachi is bigger, and Tony is the biggest.

Is Randy littler than Sachi? _____

tiny

_____

- -

_____

There are 9 girls in first grade.
A third of them wear red skirts and blue shirts.
A third of them wear red skirts and green shirts.
A third of them wear blue skirts and red shirts.

How many girls wear red skirts? _____

skirts

_____

- -

_____

We must jump through 7 hoops to finish the race.
I have already jumped through 3 hoops.

How many more hoops must I jump through? _____

hoops

_____

_____

His herd has 8 sheep.
My herd has 6 sheep.

How can we make the herds equal? _____

_____

herd

_____

- -

_____

9 people come to the dance.

Can everyone have a partner? _____

partner

_____

- -

_____

We have 8 trees in the orchard.
2 are apple trees, 3 are peach trees, and the rest are orange trees.

How many trees are orange trees? _____

orchard
_____

- -

_____

Peter has 2 sisters.
Peter's Dad gave each child in the family 3 dollars.

How many dollars did Peter's Dad give? _____

sisters

_____

- -

_____

Ducks, geese, and hens live in the barnyard.
There are 7 ducks, 8 geese, and 9 hens.

Are there more ducks than geese? _____

Are there more hens than ducks? _____

barnyard

_____

- -

_____

Cheng-kee put 9 ornaments on the tree.
The one at the top is a star.
The rest are silver balls.

How many balls are on the tree? _____

ornaments
_____

- -

_____

[blank drawing box]

The birdbath holds 9 birds.
6 birds perch on the birdbath.

How many more birds can perch on the birdbath? _____

bird

_____

- -

_____

(empty box)

The king has a golden crown.
There are 2 emeralds at each point on the crown.
The crown has 5 points.

How many emeralds are in the crown? _____

crown

_____

- -

_____

5 children sit at the table.

Mom has 9 crackers.

She gives each child the same number of crackers.

How many crackers does each child get? _____

How many crackers are left? _____

crackers

_____

- -

_____

[blank drawing box]

Pearl hikes 5 miles to the bus terminal.
Merv hikes to the terminal, and then 3 miles farther.

How many miles does Merv hike? _____

Pearl

_____

- -

_____

[blank drawing box]

Our yard is full of birds.
We have 2 robins, 3 larks, 1 warbler, and 3 sparrows.

How many birds are in the yard? _____

larks

_____

- -

_____

[blank drawing box]

Kurt needs to earn 9 dollars.
He earns 1 dollar an hour for serving meals.
He has already worked for 6 hours.

How much longer must Kurt work? _____

earn _____

_____

Ann has an allowance of 8 dollars.
She spent 3 dollars on lunches, 2 dollars on bus fare,
and 1 dollar on flowers.

How much money does she have left? _____

flowers

_____

- -

_____

_____
| |
| |
| |
| |
| |
| |
| |
| |
| |
| |
|_____|

4 five-pound blocks sit on one side of the seesaw.
6 five-pound blocks sit on the other side.

How can we make the seesaw balance? _____

_____

pound _____

- - - - - - - - - - - - - - - - - - - -

_____

Maria is putting 2 feathers on each hat.
There are 4 hats.

How many feathers? _____

feathers

_____

- -

_____

Every year Carol gets a new pearl for her necklace.
2 years ago Carol had 7 pearls in the necklace.

How old is Carol now? _____

pearls

_____

- -

_____

They played music on flutes and bugles.
7 people were playing.
4 of them played bugles.
The rest played flutes.

How many were playing flutes? _____

flutes
_____

- -

_____

Each beautiful ewe had 1 black lamb and 1 white lamb.
There were 7 ewes.

How many black lambs were there? _____

beautiful

_____

- -

_____

Planes were at the airfield.
8 planes were taking off.
6 planes were landing.

How many more planes were taking off than landing? _____

airfield

_____

- -

_____

How many shoes must you

buy for a set of quintuplets? _____

quintuplets

_____

- -

_____

Xavier bought enough apples for the class.
7 of them were ripe.
2 were still green.

How many apples did Xavier buy? _____

bought

_____

- -

_____

I saw 3 astronauts fit in each spaceship.
4 spaceships are up right now.

How many astronauts are in space right now? _____

astronauts
_____
- -
_____

[blank drawing box]

Evetta saw 6 fawns on the lawn.
When she looked again, 4 were gone.

How many fawns are still there? _____

fawn

_____

- -

_____

Draw 3 trees.
Draw the smallest one on the left.
Draw the largest one on the right.

largest

_____

- -

_____

Germaine wanted to measure the windows.
The first window was 3 feet wide.
The second window was twice as wide.

How wide was the second window? _____

measure

_____

- -

_____

In my room I have 1 bed, 3 chairs, 1 desk,
and 1 couch.

How many pieces of furniture do I have in my room? _____

furniture

_____

- -

_____

[blank box]

Marty gets sleepy at 10 o'clock.
His sister gets sleepy at 6 o'clock.

Who gets sleepy later? _____

sleepy

_____

_____

(blank box)

José and Sky try to fly the toy airplane.
It flies for the first 2 tries.
It doesn't fly the next 4 tries.

How many times did they try? _____

fly

_____

- -

_____

The cylinder on the left is 5 inches tall.
The cylinder on the right is twice as tall.

How tall is the cylinder on the right? _____

cylinder _____

_____

[blank box]

We have 2 blocks of ice on one side of the seesaw.
On the other side, we have 6 blocks of ice.
The blocks of ice each weigh the same amount.

What do we need to do to make the seesaw balance?

_____

ice _____

- -

_____

Each woman washed 2 shirts.
8 shirts are now clean.

How many women were washing? _____

women

_____

- -

_____

Sarah must unsaddle 9 horses.
She has unsaddled 5 of them.

How many horses still have saddles on? _____

unsaddle

_____

- -

_____

Using circles, squares, and triangles, make a picture
of a giraffe.

giraffe
_____

- -

_____

We have 8 lambs in our flock
We must divide the flock in half.

How many lambs will be in each half? _____

lambs, half

_____

_____

We have 8 candleholders on our chandelier.
We need new bulbs for some of them.
5 lights are still glowing.

How many new bulbs do we need? _____

chandelier

_____

- -

_____

There are 3 barns on my farm.
Bart's farm has twice as many barns.

How many barns are on Bart's farm? _____

barns

_____

- -

_____

9 friendly monsters appeared in my dream.
A friend made almost all of them disappear.
Only 1 monster was left.

How many disappeared? _____

disappear

_____

- -

_____

The bank had 9 million dollars.
One day they had a big robbery.
The robbers took a lot of money.
The bank only has 1 million dollars left.

How much money did the robbers take? _____

money _____

_____

_____

8 frogs were in the jungle.
A python ate some of them.
3 frogs are left.

How many frogs did the python eat? _____

python

_____

- -

_____

[Empty drawing box]

2 basketball teams get ready in the gym.
There are 5 women on each team.

How many women get ready to play? _____

gym _____
- -
_____

[blank box]

4 honest boys told their teacher what they
had for lunch.
John ate 5 helpings of spaghetti.
Gerry ate 3 helpings.
Sam ate 8 helpings.
Thomas ate 7 helpings.

Who ate the most? _____

honest

_____

- -

_____

My favorite TV program has 4 commercials.
Each commercial lasts 2 minutes.

How many minutes of
commercials must I sit through when
I watch my favorite program? _____

commercials

_____

- -

_____

Make a picture of 2 circles.
Divide the first circle in half.
Divide the second circle into quarters.

circle

[blank drawing box]

3 giants planted flowers.
Baby Giant planted 2 flowers.
Mother Giant planted twice as many as Baby Giant.
Father Giant planted twice as many as Mother Giant.

How many flowers did Father Giant plant? _____

giant _____

- -

_____

My room is 6 yardsticks long.
My sister's room is 2 yardsticks longer than my room.
My brother's room is half as long as my sister's room.

How long is my brother's room? _____

_____

yardstick

_____

- -

_____

3 ladies were dancing in the ballet.
Each lady had a partner.

How many people were dancing? _____

lady

_____

- -

_____

These eagles eat 3 eels at each meal.
9 eels were eaten at today's meal.

How many eagles were there? _____

eels

_____

- -

_____

Irene, Iris, and I are eating pie.
We divided the pie equally.
I took my slices first.
I have 2 slices on my plate.

How many slices are left for Irene and Iris? _____

slices

_____

- -

_____

Roland and Winona are cutting roses.
There are 7 roses on the bush.

If they cut them all, can they each
cut the same number of roses? _____

roses

_____

- -

_____

READ IT! DRAW IT! SOLVE IT! • GRADE 1

_____

I planted tulips so that they would bloom in a pattern.
The pattern is red, orange, yellow, red, orange, yellow.

What color is the fifth tulip? _____

What color is the ninth tulip? _____

tulip

_____

- -

_____

[blank drawing box]

I am cutting fruit into cubes to make a nice dessert.
10 cubes are already cut.
I is peach, 2 are orange, 4 are apple, and the rest
are melon cubes.

How many melon cubes have been cut? _____

cubes

_____

- -

_____

_____

Our band has only flutes, tubas, and trumpets.
There are the same number of each instrument in the band.
We have 9 instruments in all.

How many tubas do we have? _____

tubas

_____

- -

_____

We are going to have a canoe race.
The blue team has 4 canoes.
The yellow team has 2 canoes.
The green team has 3 canoes.

How can we make the teams equal? _____

_____

canoe

_____

- -

_____

Make a picture of a circle.
Divide the circle into 2 equal parts.
Color the left half red.
Color the right half blue.

circle

_____

- -

_____

Here is Ruth's math paper.
It has 4 addition problems.
It has 2 division problems.
She got 2 problems wrong.
All the rest are right.

How many did she get right? _____

division

_____

- -

_____

8 two-ton elephants sit on the left side of the seesaw.
6 two-ton elephants sit on the right side of the seesaw.

How can we make the seesaw balance? _____

_____

elephant _____

- -

_____

We have an orchestra at our school.
2 people are playing the violin.
Twice as many people are playing the trumpet.

How many people are playing the trumpet? _____

orchestra

_____

- -

_____